L♥VE *in a* LUNCH BOX

L♥VE in a LUNCH BOX

101 SUGGESTIONS FOR HAPPIER, HEALTHIER LUNCHES

BY CAROLE RAYMOND

Beautiful America Publishing Company

Library of Congress Catalog Card Number 94-27382
ISBN 0-89802-616-4

Published by **Beautiful America Publishing**©
P.O. Box 646, Wilsonville, Oregon 97070
503-682-0173

Author: Carole Raymond
Foreword: Ron Jones
Illustrator: Kit Raymond
Design: Heather Kier

Printed in Korea

Dedication

For Dick Raymond, forever.

Table of Contents

Foreword

My wife once sent me a message of dire importance. It was stuffed in my lunch bag, wrapped around a sandwich—one raunchy gym sock. Yuk! I got the message. In fact I almost ate it. From that moment on I always looked at my lunch as a source for subtle reminders, romantic invitations or Euclidian problems. Yes, my socks found their way from under the bed to the washing machine.

Love in a Lunch Box gives parents the ideas and recipes to make their child's lunch not only nutritious but an important part of family life. As fast food marketing takes over the food selection at the supermarket, replaces the local restaurant, and even invades the school kitchen, *Love in a Lunch Box* gives the parent and child a way to reclaim what they eat and why they eat it! There are lots of wonderful food selections from *Monster Treats* to *Ants on a Log* to *Rainbow Drinks*. Simple descriptions on how to make a *Floppy Disc Pizza*, *Sweet Pea Dip*, and *Jicama Orange Mint Salad*. But most important of all *Love in a Lunch Box* gives doable advice to families for spending time together around the preparation and enjoyment of our daily lunch.

The one problem with reading this book is that I'm getting hungry and thinking about what I can put in my granddaughter's lunch bag to remind her of how much I love her. So find out all about food treasure events, secret messages and *Gorilla Grahams* for as Carole Raymond reminds us…

"Above all, enjoy your children
for these days once gone,
can never be recaptured."

Ron Jones

Acknowledgments

Ursula and Thorn Bacon, Roberta Miller,

Roberta Gross, Betty Temple, Anna Beck, Katie Beck,

Nancy Byles, Ted and Beverly Paul,

Nancy Hankins, Heather Kier

About the Book

Millions of kids leave for school each morning. They pile into buses and automobiles; some ride bikes, others walk. Whatever their mode of transportation, most children arrive at their destination toting lunch boxes in every imaginable shape and color. Although the superheroes and super-heroines who decorate the sides of the lunch box have changed through the years, the problem of what to pack has not.

Countless articles in national publications continue to warn the American public about the hazards of eating fat-laden food. Research shows children as young as three years old can display the first signs of elevated cholesterol levels in their blood. Recent studies confirm forty percent of school-age children already carry at least one risk factor for heart disease. Helping children establish smart eating habits at an early age helps pave the road for future good health. No matter what a child's background risk or cholesterol level may be, parents would do well to start reducing the amount of fat in their diets.

Like no other book, *Love in a Lunch Box* offers a multitude of fresh lunch-packing ideas guaranteed not to be dumped into overflowing garbage cans or into dark hall lockers. In this book, parents can choose foods high in complex carbohydrates, such as whole grains, pasta, rice, beans, cereal, bread, fresh fruits, and vegetables.

The daily race to work and school forces families to say goodbye at sunrise, not to meet again until sunset. Parents are looking for ways to connect with their children during the long hours spent apart.

In the chapter "Pack Magic in the Morning," special attention is given to 100 whimsical ideas parents can use to say "I love you" at lunchtime. Suggestions as simple as packing a banana-gram, a message written on the peel of a banana, keeps parents and children in touch.

Love in a Lunch Box is packed with solutions to the many concerns parents voice daily:

- What can I pack for lunch today?

- How can I reduce the amount of fat my child eats?

- How can I help my teenager cut down on junk food?

- How can I help my child develop a taste for nutritious food?

- What can I pack for my overweight child?

- How can I help my children pack their own lunches?

- How can I prepare lunches that get my child's attention?

- What can I do to prevent the mad-morning lunch-packing rush?

- What can I prepare the night before that will stay fresh?

- Where can I find simple, reusable packing supplies?
  How do I keep them handy?

- How can I save time and money?

- How can I say "I love you?"

These questions and many more are answered in clever, imaginative ways. More than forty cartoon illustrations and a delightful selection of humorous anecdotes lighten the daily lunch-packing chore. This book is a unique, practical guide to better lunches.

Eating
Styles

CHAPTER 1

We all have our particular eating styles and personal preferences, and children are no exception. If you have a child who isn't picky about food, you're lucky. Most of us have the other kind. For many children, a balanced meal means carrying lunch boxes on their heads without dropping them.

Typically, there are those children who use the "dessert-first" approach at lunchtime. Their radar vision zaps to the sweet treat packed at the bottom of the lunch box. The half-eaten sandwich is brought home crusts intact, to be fed to the family goldfish, with the excuse "But I only had time to eat the cookies."

For other children, lunch is a disappearing act. The clever young Houdini first drinks the milk and then stuffs whatever is green or mushy into the empty milk carton and tosses it with precision into the garbage can. For the athletically inclined, lunch takes on the excitement of the hundred-meter dash. Lunch is left behind, for the race is to see who can get to the playground first.

There are exceptions to the rule for the run to recess. Occasionally, there is a child who likes to linger over lunch. The school-cafeteria cooks found Henry taking his time. He changed jackets with friends and borrowed eyeglasses; and with his new costume, he sneaked back to the lunch line for seconds and even thirds.

With so many things that can go wrong at lunchtime, parents sometimes feel that the "best" lunch is simply one that their child will eat. But that may not be the best solution. There are ways to negotiate answers that are acceptable to both parent and child.

When lunch turns into a swap meet, and the crisp carrot sticks and juicy oranges you packed in the morning are traded for a hunk of lazy-dazey cake or even a baseball card or two at noon, you can do something about it. Offer to include items in your child's lunch box that can be exchanged without giving up the fruit and vegetables you want them to eat.

While parents may worry about nutrition, children worry about fitting in with friends. Although your child might like prunes, if friends consider them weird your child will not eat them at school. Try packing something else. If classmates choose lettuce on their sandwiches, you may find sprouts are out.

It is wise to pay attention to children's food choices or you might make a discovery like a friend of mine did. While cleaning her son's room, she found his winter boots stuffed with the sprouts she had packed in his school lunches.

Almost all children go through food phases of some kind. My son who doesn't like chicken, fish, or beef tells me, "Mom, I'm a vegetarian who doesn't like vegetables." If your child is healthy, don't worry. This month's phase will pass.

One mother complained to me that her children are as picky as the birds in her yard that carefully choose their favorite morsels from the bird seed she scatters, leaving the rest to mold on the ground.

Some problems are common among children. Remember that young children don't want to cope with anything too complicated. Help your child do something better than play the lunchtime garbage can game of "basketball" with whole apples and oranges being the ball. Shop for small apples for small children, or cut a big apple in half and rub it with lemon juice to keep it from turning a suspicious color. Peeling oranges can be a difficult task for small fingers, so score the skin with a knife, or pack peeled oranges.

The haphazard eating styles of adolescents seem to be a part of growing up and the search for independence. Skipped meals, crash diets, snacking on empty calories, and fast-food dining leave parents spinning. The best thing you can do is to make the right kinds of food available at home. Nutritious food that is refrigerator-ready for lunches and snacks will help you compete with cleverly packaged junk food.

Children like making choices. School lunch programs take advantage of this trait and find their sales increase when they allow students to select the items they prefer. (Traditionally, school-cafeteria trays are served with all the choices made by the cook.) When packing lunch at home, the final vote as to what goes into the bag can belong to your child. Picking what to eat seems to make things taste better.

The issue of the ballooning lunchtime garbage can continues from kindergarten through graduate school. My child's first-grade teacher tried solving the problem with a subsidized lunch program of her own. The food her students refused to eat was put in a cardboard box in front of the room. The class could then go to the box and pick out what they wanted from their friends' rejects. Some mothers avoided packing lunch all year as their children took advantage of this plan.

Remember that styles are subject to change. What your child refuses today may become tomorrow's favorite choice.

To Help Ease Lunch-Packing Frustrations

- Stock your refrigerator with nutritious food.

- Keep the food you pack simple.

- Pay attention to the peer pressure your child faces.

- Let children help plan lunch-box menus.

- Keep laughing and enjoy the changes.

Pack Magic in the Morning

Julie rode to school in her pony cart and carried her lunch. She lived near the city dump where her father was the gatekeeper. Each afternoon when Julie unpacked her lunch, she found a napkin on which her father had drawn a picture for her. Julie told me this story when she was eighty years old. Often, it is the small things we do for our children that are most remembered.

Perusing the refrigerator at 6:00 a.m. for lunchtime inspiration is, admittedly, difficult. The morning rush usually leaves little time for extras. On those mornings when the clock forgets to run on fast forward, use the ideas in this chapter to turn plain brown bags and dented lunch boxes into something to remember.

Gratifying Goodies

■ Write an invitation to an upcoming event. "The pleasure of your company is requested for a trip to the movies this Saturday night."

■ Clip a cartoon from a newspaper or magazine. Replace the comment in the talk-bubble with one of your own.

■ Tuck in a love note. "Have a nice day." "You're a great kid." "Good luck on your spelling test." Write your note on a napkin or buy yourself a notepad and keep it near your packing supplies.

■ Send a countdown reminder to a special event. "Only five more days until B-day" (birthday). Continue the countdown until blastoff.

■ Pack a recess game like jacks, pick-up sticks, or a small jigsaw puzzle. Make a simple puzzle by cutting up a picture postcard. Send it in a baggie for lunchtime assembling.

■ Send the "Blue Ribbon" special. Stop by your local trophy

and ribbon store. Buy a few first-place blue ribbons to slip into the lunch box to say "You're a Winner!"

■ Design a certificate of acknowledgment for a job well done. "To Jonathan, the Golden Wheels Bicycle Award, member of the two-wheeler club."

■ Draw your own cartoon character. Even if you think you can't draw, your child will enjoy your hilarious attempt.

■ Buy a package of fortune cookies. It is sometimes possible to slip your own message into the cookie.

■ For your teenager, buy an inexpensive horoscope book and send a weekly prediction, or clip the horoscope from the newspaper.

■ Tuck in a newspaper clipping or short magazine article of special interest.

■ Celebrate the day by sending a piece of cake labeled "Happy Unbirthday."

■ In spring, after the last frost, put a few sunflower seeds in an envelope with the following directions: "Here are some seeds. I hope not weeds. What could they be? Plant them and see. In a sunny spot in the garden, plant these seeds one-half inch deep and one foot apart. Water once or twice a week."

■ Buy a magazine subscription for your child. Send a card announcing the subscription in the lunch box.

■ Arrange a lunch swap. If someone else's mother or father makes lunch, it might taste even better.

■ Consider a lunch-box holiday. Send a Chinese treat on Chinese New Year's, or a special Valentine's Day lunch.

■ Holidays are important markers of time for children. Take advantage of those days in your family's traditions. Send a special-occasion card to your child, c/o the Lunch Box.

■ Tuck in a fresh flower wrapped in a plastic baggie with a few droplets of water to keep it fresh.

■ Pack a treat wrapped and labeled "To share with a friend."

■ Buy extra Valentine's cards and slip one into the lunch box occasionally.

■ Run an ad in the classified section for your child. "To Tom, our high-point man. We love you." Send the ad in the lunch.

■ Send a treasure map with instructions such as "When you get home, look under your pillow." (Under the pillow, put directions to the next hiding place. Continue the clues until your child is led to a surprise.)

■ Send a sticker for collecting or a lapel button with a favorite saying or picture.

■ Buy an inexpensive copy of *The Guinness Book of Records*. Select an item each week, and send this "Incredible Inedible" to read at lunchtime.

■ Pack a throwaway moist paper towel on the day you pack a hearty "hands-on" lunch.

■ Send a photo from a newly developed roll of film, or an old favorite for your child to share with a friend during lunchtime. Send it slipped between two pieces of cardboard in an envelope labeled "Handle with Care."

■ Send pretzels or raisins in a sealed, colored envelope.

■ Tuck in a small gift such as colorful shoelaces, hair clips, an eraser, a bookmark, or a personalized notepad or pencil.

■ Tape record jokes or riddles or a story. Announce the tape with a note: "When you get home from school today, turn on the tape recorder."

■ Collect your own set of trivia cards and send "The Trivia Question of the Week."

■ For the young child who is learning to read, buy a children's poetry book and send a "Poem of the Week."

■ Add a fancy napkin, doily, or straw. Try tucking in an inexpensive cloth napkin for a touch of distinction.

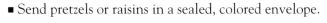
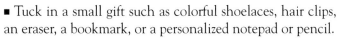

■ Design a coupon for redemption such as "This coupon entitles you to breakfast in bed Sunday morning."

■ Wrap a sandwich in recycled birthday or holiday paper.

■ Surprise your teenager with a box of animal crackers.

■ Decorate a paper lunch sack with felt pens, crayons, rubber stamps, or stickers. Occasionally buy a "designer" lunch bag from your local stationery store.

■ Buy an ink stamp with your child's name on it. You can mark the lunch sack, and your child can have fun using the stamp.

Food for Thought

■ Send a "Word-of-the-Week." By the time your child graduates from high school, you may have introduced over 500 new words to his or her vocabulary.

■ For a young child, buy a dot-to-dot book and a book of mazes. Send a clipped page for lunchtime fun.

■ Buy an inexpensive riddle and joke book and send one riddle or joke each week. Here are a few to get you started: "What is the best thing to put into a cookie?" (Your teeth.) "What has many teeth but can't bite?" (A comb.) "What always wakes up with its shoes on?" (A horse.)

■ Pack a lunch-box mystery. Print a note backward. Send along instructions saying, "Can you figure out this message? Hold it up to a mirror for decoding." Or use this vowel code for a secret sentence: A=!, E=#, i=$, o=%, u=&. L#t's r#nt ! v$d#% t%n$ght. Have fun inventing loads of codes.

Handle Familiar Foods with Flourish

■ Surprise your child with "flamingo eggs." Peel hard-cooked eggs and cut them in half. Discard cholesterol-filled yolks. Soak the egg whites in the juice that has been drained from a can of beets for about fifteen minutes. Refill the egg hollow with this garbanzo bean spread. With a fork, mash together 2 Tb. canned garbanzo beans, 2 tsp. liquid from canned beans, 1 tsp. Dijon mustard, 1 tsp. minced parsley.

■ Make an orange fruit cup. Slice the top off an orange and save it. Scoop out the contents of the orange and mix orange pieces with sliced bananas, grapes, or chopped apples. Return the mixture to the hollowed-out orange, put on the lid, and wrap. At Halloween, add a face made out of whole cloves.

■ Save some Easter grass from your child's Easter basket. Use the grass occasionally as a nest for an apple, radishes, or green grapes.

■ Send an apple puzzle. This idea will put apples on the top of your child's favorite-foods list. Pack an extra puzzle, because your child's friends will want one too. Make this puzzle with just four easy cuts. With the apple stem pointing up, use a sharp 4-to-6-inch-long knife and cut down halfway through the apple. Turn the apple upside down, blossom end up. Position the knife at a right angle to the first cut. Again, cut halfway through the apple. At point "A," insert the knife to the core, and cut along the equator to point "B." Remove the knife. At point "C," insert the knife to the core, and cut along the equator to point "D." Remove the knife. Pull the apple apart. Hooray, you did it! Put the halves together, and pack for lunch.

  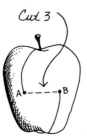 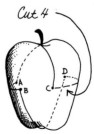

Cut 1   Cut 2   Cut 3   Cut 4

■ Put popcorn in a homemade paper cone and cover with plastic wrap. To make a cone, cut a triangle or pie slice out of a circle and fold the cut circle into a cone. Although children might think popcorn is the invention of movie theaters, the Indians of Peru were popping corn more than 1,000 years ago. American Indians believed the popping was caused by a demon imprisoned inside the corn kernel. The demon is actually a combination of tightly packed starch and the right amount of moisture. When the popcorn kernel is heated, the water trapped inside becomes steam and explodes the kernel. Send popcorn that has been air popped and avoid heavily oiled commercial brands.

■ Send melon balls sprinkled with minced parsley.

■ Pack a banana-gram. Use a dark felt pen or ball-point pen to write a message on the peel of a banana, or draw eyes and a mouth on the banana to make a banana slug.

Who Said Vegetables Aren't Any Fun?

There is no limit to the vegetable game.

■ Assemble veggie and fruit kabobs. Cut vegetables or fruit into bite-sized pieces and skewer them on teriyaki sticks. Rub fruit with lemon juice to avoid discoloration.

■ Make a veggie go-cart. Cut four carrot rounds for wheels and attach them with toothpicks to a 3-to-4-inch-long celery stalk. Stuff celery with a favorite sandwich spread.

■ Add a line of raisins to some stuffed celery to look like ants on a log, or sprinkle stuffed celery with grated carrots or chopped green pepper to look like confetti.

■ Create veggie characters. Cut celery into about 4-inch lengths. Fill cavity with a sandwich spread. Use a piece of celery with green leaves still attached or use alfalfa sprouts for hair, raisin eyes, radish lips, or a cashew mouth, and attach carrot rounds with toothpicks for ears.

- Create vegetable "cookies." With a cookie cutter, cut various shapes from thin slices of cooked beets or raw turnips.

- Send zucchini flowers. With a sharp knife, score zucchini lengthwise. Cuts should be 1/4 inch apart and 1/8 inch deep. Next, cut the vegetable crosswise into 1/2 inch slices. Send along a container of dip.

- Make a veggie satellite-kabob. Place a radish between two cucumber rounds. Slip onto a toothpick and add a carrot chunk to each side to hold cucumber in the center of the toothpick.

- Do something as simple as decorating the ends of carrot sticks with dates or prunes.

Pack an Edible Container

- Send "Baked Ice Cream." Prepare a cake batter. Set a flat-bottomed ice cream cone in each cup of a muffin tin. Fill the cones three-quarters full with cake batter. Bake the cones for about thirty minutes. Test them to see if they are done by poking a toothpick into the cake. If the toothpick comes out clean, the cake is done. Let cool and pack for lunch.

- Create a lettuce-leaf package. Use a large pliable leaf of Boston lettuce. Spread a favorite sandwich filling on the bottom third of the lettuce leaf. Next, roll up the leaf with the mixture inside. Secure with a toothpick if necessary.

- Send a green potato. Slice a baked potato in half. Scoop the insides into a blender with 1/2 cup leftover cooked broccoli or spinach. Add a splash of non-fat milk or water and a dash of salt and pepper. Whirl in a blender and return the mixture to the shell.

- Send a rosy-red potato. Slice a baked potato in half while it is still warm. Scoop out the insides and mash with a fork. Add a splash of liquid drained from a can of beets. Sprinkle with a shake of dill, salt, and pepper. Mix until smooth. Return mixture to potato shell. Chill and wrap for lunch.

- Pack an egg cup. Cut the tip off a hard-cooked egg. Scoop out the yolk and discard it. Fill the cavity with a favorite sandwich filling. Replace the tip and wrap.

■ Make a pepper pot. Hollow out a green pepper and fill it with your child's favorite salad.

■ Stuff hollowed-out cherry tomatoes or snow-pea pods with a favorite sandwich spread.

Set Your Imagination Free Making Sandwiches and Enjoy Yourself

■ Sponsor a family sandwich-making contest and offer a grand prize for the "notable totable."

■ Cut out a heart shape from slices of bread on Valentine's Day or any day that you want to say "I Love You." Try triangles, a circle, or a triple-decker.

■ Make a sleeping-bag sandwich. Trim the crusts, flatten the slice of bread with a rolling pin, spread with filling, roll, secure with a toothpick, and wrap.

■ Pack sandwich halves with different fillings.

■ Use a cookie cutter to cut a heart from the center of the top slice of sandwich bread and let the filling show.

■ Use two kinds of bread in one sandwich.

■ Label a sandwich after a favorite character such as The "Bugs Bunny" Special.

■ Make an "open-faced" sandwich. Cut your bread into a circle. Spread it with a favorite filling and add a face with raisins, carrot slices, etc. Wrap in plastic.

■ Choose two different kinds of bread. Use a cookie cutter to cut out the same shape from each slice of bread. Then insert each cut-out design into the opposite slice of bread.

Smart
Choices

CHAPTER 3

Highlighting wholesome eating is more important than haranguing a child about what not to eat. Parents can begin helping their children by "fat-proofing" the kitchen: stock the cupboards and refrigerator with whole grains, pasta, rice, cereal, bread, beans, fresh fruit, and vegetables. Helping your child establish smart eating habits today paves the road for future good health.

If you are making major alterations in your child's diet, introduce food changes gradually. You want to create a workable harmony between what exists and any shifts that need to be made. New eating patterns that are introduced within your child's current eating habits are likely to be successful.

Little Inventions Make a Big Difference

■ Be aware of the fat-filled, sugar-packed desserts of the marketplace. These "little" pies, cupcakes, and other such creations can add empty calories and fat to a meal.

■ Use unadorned and unfilled cookies or unfrosted cupcakes and muffins for dessert. Bake small cookies. A simple dessert does much toward making a child feel well fed.

■ If your child is a "muncher," replace fat-laden potato chips with a bag of unsalted air-popped corn. Use baked chips instead of fried.

■ Instead of spreading a sandwich with butter and mayonnaise, which are loaded with fat, use mustard.

■ Non-fat yogurt or applesauce instead of fat-filled mayonnaise can be used as a binder for various sandwich fillings.

■ When making sandwiches, use whole-grain bread, which is naturally full of vitamins and fiber.

■ Choose fresh fruits and vegetables rather than the sugar-sweetened canned or processed equivalents.

■ Avoid highly processed meat products, particularly meat spreads, as they tend to be high in fat.

■ Search out creative low-fat recipes. There are many excellent recipes that don't require exotic preparation.

Do not become an obsessive fat-gram counter. Do invest in a good book that outlines nutritive values and use it to learn the general composition of favorite foods and to find alternatives for high-fat foods. *Food Values of Portions Commonly Used*, by Pennington and Church, is an excellent resource book.

Teenagers generally have ravenous appetites because of the growth that occurs during adolescence. Don't lecture on how much your children seem to eat at home, instead provide nutritious food choices when filling your grocery cart. When your child is at school, discourage skipping lunch since this causes low energy and inability to concentrate. The food missed in skipped meals is almost always made up, and then some, by eating high-fat snacks.

Most children are "snackers." This is a natural pattern with growing children who sometimes eat as much as thirty-five percent of their daily food from snacks. However, if your child is excessively hungry between meals, check to see if meals contain enough whole grains, fresh fruits, and vegetables, which provide the "staying" power between meals.

Just because a food sounds healthy doesn't mean that it is. Take a moment to read the labels of the prepared foods you buy. Some non-fat products are high in sugar and loaded with chemicals, which you may wish to avoid.

Check the serving size described on the label. If a brownie mix says it has only two grams of fat for each serving, but the brownie is one inch by one inch, I know my child could devour six servings without taking a breath between bites. I'll probably choose something else. When choosing among brands of packaged or canned food, read competitors' labels. Although the food may be the same, the amount of salt, sugar, fat, and the number of artificial additives can vary greatly among available choices.

Sometimes two foods can have the same basic ingredients, but one has less fat than the other because of the way it is prepared. Look for foods that are baked, not fried. Here is a chart to help you pick the food with more nutritional value.

Sounds Healthy	Is Healthy
2% milk	Non-fat milk
Granola	Oatmeal
Iceberg lettuce	Dark-green leafy vegetables
French fries	Baked potato
Breakfast bar	High-fiber cereal, fruit, non-fat milk
Store-bought popcorn	Air-popped popcorn
Deep-fried potato chips	Baked chips and fat-free pretzels
Orange drink	Orange juice
Granola bar	Fat-free Fig Newton
Banana chips	Banana
Low-fat yogurt	Non-fat yogurt
Yogurt- or chocolate-covered raisins	Raisins
Whole eggs	Egg whites

While living in Alaska, one second-grade student had a teacher who fed the class a daily dose of vitamins. Each child kept a spoon inside his or her desk. At the appointed hour, the teacher lined the class up in front of her desk and uncapped a bottle of cod liver oil and filled each spoon with the terrible-tasting liquid. Spare your child the need for that memorable taste, and instead pack foods that are full of vitamins and essential minerals.

Current research reports children getting fatter. One-third of all teenage girls are on diets. Diets are not the answer for growing children. Food that is low in fat and high in complex carbohydrates is good for all children and can benefit overweight children especially.

Another important thing parents can do for their children is to get them moving. Fitness experts agree that children are likely to develop lifelong fitness habits if they are introduced to healthy activities early on. Researchers have discovered that physical activity helps reduce body fat as well as raise the level of HDL protective cholesterol. Discuss with your child's P.E. teacher the opportunities available at school. Many schools schedule after-school athletic programs. Some programs provide non-competitive choices such as jump-rope drill teams and marching teams. Teenagers can also take advantage of after-school clubs such as cycling and cross-country skiing.

Help young children organize swimming, roller-skating, and ice-skating parties with friends. Jazzercise, tap dancing, and square dancing are popular activities. Check in with your local YMCA and municipal recreation departments and see what exercise programs they offer.

Kids who feel embarrassingly uncoordinated at organized sports can jog and walk without shame. The only equipment they need is a pair of good running shoes. While studies show that adults are exercising more, kids are exercising less. Take advantage of this fact, and exercise with your child. Go for a walk together and enjoy a simple, inexpensive pleasure of being a parent.

Notable Totables

CHAPTER 4

Carrying a lunch box to school is an exciting event for a young child. It symbolizes graduation from kindergarten and membership into the fraternity of "big kids." For some children, carrying the lunch box is even more important than what's inside. I know a first-grader who refused to eat anything his mother packed, and, nevertheless, insisted on carrying an empty lunch box each day.

Young children like carrying lunch boxes advertising current superheroes and superheroines, and the lunch-box hall of fame is filled with a collection of stars. If your child's lunch box is out of date, try adding a few stickers to last year's model. Children enjoy individualizing their belongings and displaying their bumper-sticker slogans. This maneuver may save you the expense of buying a new lunch box.

Older children prefer carrying lunch bags–anonymous carriers without their names written across them. Then, if they accidentally forget to throw their bags into the garbage, the litter remains circumstantial evidence, and the offenders go free.

The lunch packers' tools have changed over the years. Before modern packaging was on the shelf of every home, children found their lunches bundled in newspaper and wrapped with string. Sandwiches were sent in old bread wrappers or had no wrapping at all.

Today, technology provides you with a medley of zip-lock bags, plastic, cardboard, and cold packs to keep warm food warm and cold food cold. Fifty years ago, before all of these inventions, Ted trudged to school on cold winter mornings through soggy snow and ice. Upon arrival, the teacher required her students to line their dripping rubber boots along the back wall of the classroom near the stove. Lunches were parked on the tops of the overshoes. While the boots slowly dried, the lunches were steamed. By noontime, the food tasted like a feast of cooked galoshes. The warm, moist smell of mingling aromas that parents recall from opening their own school lunches can now be chilled, separated, and sealed in plastic.

It is an easy task to equip yourself with a collection of sturdy serving-size containers to use in lunch packing. Like coat hangers in the closet, reusable tins and cartons from commercial packing seem to multiply by themselves in the cupboard. They make lightweight carriers for lunch-box toting and are more likely to be brought home than your new Tupperware. A good place to buy inexpensive, recycled packing supplies is at your local church rummage sale or thrift shop.

Save your silverware from being lost by adding a few inexpensive plastic spoons and forks to your packing supplies. Toothpicks can sometimes serve in place of a fork and can transform simple fare like sliced vegetables into hors d'oeuvres; or consider investing in sturdy camping-style silverware. Children might enjoy the novelty.

Some children are willing to carry lunch packing paraphernalia to and from school, and others are not. There are those who prefer to grow penicillin mold in forgotten jars stuffed into the dark corners of their desks. Don't burden children with too many supplies to bring home. If you send a favorite from your collection and worry that you won't get it back, try offering a small reward for its return like supermarkets do for pop bottles.

One of the last things a parent wants to receive is a phone call from the school nurse with the message "Your child is here with a stomachache." Make sure whatever goes into the lunch box is clean. If you pack lunch in a paper bag, use a fresh one. Oil-stained bags with bits of decomposing food are the breeding ground for contamination. Reuse tin foil and plastic bags at home in your refrigerator, but avoid reusing them in unrefrigerated lunch boxes unless they are scrubbed clean of yesterday's food. Wash plastic food containers and lunch boxes in very hot water after each use.

There need be nothing haphazard in your lunch packing. Set aside a shelf in your cupboard to hold packing supplies, and keep your cupboard well stocked to save time and tempers in the midst of the morning rush. Armed with the proper equipment, you can pack the lunch box quickly and victoriously.

The lunch may have a difficult journey. If it's stuffed into a backpack or dropped while waiting for the bus, used for a punching bag or bowling ball, it might not look the same at lunchtime as when it left home. Use plastic containers to protect fragile food, pack heavy things on the bottom of the bag, and hope for the best.

Some Like It Hot, Some Like It Cold

In Ireland, my friend Sue and her classmates carted their milk to school in empty catsup bottles and occasionally in a blue Milk of Magnesia bottle. The milk was set by the coal-burning fireplace to warm. One happy child was given the job of rotating the bottles throughout the cold winter morning. The lucky milk monitor was also warmed by the fireside job. If the child forgot to turn the bottles, which sometimes happened, he or she risked the disaster of exploding milk missiles.

Nowadays, vacuum bottles are one solution to temperature control, and your child need not worry about spilled milk. Store vacuum-bottle lid and cup separately from the bottle itself to prevent odors from developing inside the container. If odors already exist, rinse the bottle in a solution of baking soda and warm water.

Cool the lunch with your own homemade freezer packs.

■ Freeze cartons of non-fat yogurt, six-ounce cans of natural juice, or small leakproof containers filled with your own blend of juice. Pack them frozen. Put them in a plastic bag to keep the moisture that accumulates in the defrosting from soaking the lunch. They will be defrosted by lunchtime and will keep the lunch cool.

■ Pack a closed plastic container filled with ice cubes to keep the lunch cool, and the melting ice will then serve as a refreshing drink of water with lunch.

■ Chill fruits and vegetables overnight before packing. When packed, they will help cool the lunch bag. If you get the jump on lunch packing by doing it the first thing in the morning, don't leave packed lunches, ready for takeoff, sitting on your kitchen counter. Keep cold items in the refrigerator and pack them at the last minute. If you worry about a meat sandwich spoiling, make it the night before and freeze it, leaving out vegetable garnishes that do not freeze well. Your child can toss it all into the lunch box before dashing out the door.

■ Use a narrow-mouthed thermos bottle for drinks.

■ Pre-chill vacuum containers in the refrigerator overnight, uncovered when packing cold drinks.

■ Avoid using glass-lined containers that can break on the sometimes bumpy trip to the lunch room.

■ Wash vacuum bottles in very hot water after each use. Freshen the bottles periodically by filling them with boiling water and adding a spoonful of baking soda. After ten minutes, rinse the bottles with clear water and store them without their lids. Opening a vacuum jar can be a job that calls for the strength of Superwoman. It seems as if the lids are tightened by an invisible hand while being carried. Many a young child has been forced, with pleading eyes, to ask the teacher, "Can you open this?" There are now vacuum bottles with a flip-top button in the cap. They have become popular with the younger set because they are easy to open.

Get Kids into the Act

One of the great pleasures of being the family lunch packer is not being the family lunch packer every now and then. This is a job that can easily be shared, for there's plenty of work for everyone. Most kids are eager kitchen helpers. Young children enjoy stirring and spreading sandwich fixings. Washing carrots and drying lettuce is a job even a five-year-old can happily do. Foods prepared by kids themselves rarely go uneaten. For kids who balk at making lunches, try the old Tom Sawyer maneuver. The lunch packer who dances and sings about the work and makes it look like fun might find everyone trying to get on stage. When given the opportunity to prepare their food, children sometimes become more adventuresome in trying new tastes. Why, they might even try escargot if they could display the shells around their necks. A high-school French teacher I know bestows this badge of courage upon her students on "International Food Day." They string the shells on a piece of twine and wear them.

Take advantage of the daily plundering of the kitchen that occurs during the teenage years. Stock your kitchen with nutritious food and make it easy for your teenagers to graze and pack lunch at the same time.

Wave goodbye to the morning rush by encouraging your child to pack as much of the lunch box as possible the night before. If you have more than one child, suggest they rotate the packing responsibility.

Eating Lunch with Braces on Your Teeth

In junior high school there can be special lunchtime problems for those children who wear braces on their teeth. Children can find eating uncomfortable while wearing a retainer, and although most dentists warn their patients to keep the appliance in place, they are often taken out at lunchtime and wrapped in a napkin for comfort, aesthetics, and safekeeping.

A thirteen-year-old, looking at a retainer sitting by a sandwich on the lunch-room table, finds it as appetizing as a thirty-year-old who discovers a set of false teeth used as the dining centerpiece. When luncheon scraps are tossed, the napkin and retainer often accidentally disappear into the garbage. If your child has a friend who also wears braces, there is an additional threat. I know two girls who inadvertently traded napkins and wore the wrong retainer. Many frustrated parents and school custodians have been seen foraging through the garbage cans after school looking for the lost piece of equipment. One junior high school launched an advertising campaign and posted signs by the garbage cans that warned, "Keep Your Retainer in Its Container–Use Your Mouth."

Losing a retainer is an expensive mistake. To help prevent the problem, ask your child to put the retainer in his or her school locker before going into the lunchroom and replace it immediately after lunch, or send a bright plastic soap dish, the kind you find in traveling cases, to hold the retainer at the lunchroom table. Help your child establish a habit of putting the retainer in the same safe place, whether it be a locker, soap dish, pocket, purse, or backpack.

Some children are so sensitive about the problem of food caught in the front of their braces that they refuse to eat at school. For those children, whip up a "bionic" shake in your blender, and send it in a vacuum bottle for lunchtime sipping. See Chapter 8 for recipe ideas.

Brushing your teeth at school isn't considered "cool" unless your father is a dentist. Help your child relax and enjoy eating lunch by adding a folding travel toothbrush and a small container of tooth-picks to the school supplies. The toothbrush and toothpicks can be kept in a locker to use for a quick "dusting" in case of an emergency.

The Star of the Lunch Box

CHAPTER 5

The sandwich is the star of the lunch box and only habit and convention keep us from trying something new. Roberta became the star of her class with the unconventional sandwiches her father packed —"chocolate goop" spread between slices of white bread. She quickly tired of this monstrous treat, but found it had great trade-in value with her friends. (Roberta grew up to become a gourmet natural-foods cook.) When you break your sandwich-making routine, have fun inventing nutritious sandwiches, and build them with a free and happy hand.

Sensational Sandwiches

In creating sandwiches, good bread is the starting point. Bakers are baking as fast as they can, and the bread rack is full of choices. Make everyday sandwiches special with special breads. Buy hearty, whole-grain loaves that are packed with nutrition, such as sesame crunch, sunflower, double bran, honey-wheat, seven- and nine-grain, sprouted wheat, oat, and whole-wheat French. Quick breads like banana, date, or gingerbread add sweetness to a sandwich. Try corn bread and raisin bread. Bagels, muffins, rolls, rice cakes, chapatis, crackers, leftover waffles, rolled pancakes, and even French toast make interesting sandwiches. Stuff a pocket bread. It's great for kids' sandwiches, for the filling won't fall out.

Buy a variety of breads to use during the week. Store them in your freezer to ensure their freshness. Spreading fillings on frozen bread makes it easier to avoid tearing the slices, and the chilled bread helps to cool the spread.

If you find yourself with dried-out bread, a light steaming has an extraordinary capacity to revive it. Wrap bread slices, pocket bread, or whatever in a tea towel and place in a steamer over gently boiling water. In a minute or two, you'll have pliable tasty bread once again. You can use a microwave to freshen baked goods by heating them inside a slightly moist paper bag on medium for 20-30 seconds.

Use the main and side dishes you customarily prepare for dinner as sandwich fillings. Think of chili and baked or non-fat refried beans as ready-made stuffings for pocket bread.

Bulk up sandwiches with extra lettuce, tomato, sprouts, and other vegetables. Turn over a new leaf, and add greens to sandwich fillings for a crunchy contrast. Try using Boston, oak leaf, romaine, and dark green, bronze, and red varieties. Endive, escarole, kale, mustard greens, turnip greens, and spinach add new tastes to sandwiches.

Sandwich Spreads Should Be Moist Enough to Be Good Without Being Wet and Drippy

If your child complains of soggy sandwiches, send an especially wet filling in a container so it can be assembled into a sandwich at lunchtime. Juicy garnishes such as sliced tomatoes can be packed separately and added to the sandwich when it's time to eat. Toasting bread adds crunch to the sandwich and helps reduce a soggy texture.

Although sandwiches taste best when freshly made, it may be necessary to make them ahead of time and freeze them for future use. Make only enough sandwiches for a week at a time, for sandwiches frozen longer begin to lose their flavor.

Know the ABCs of Successful Sandwich Freezing

■ Carefully wrap sandwiches that are to be frozen in heavy freezer paper that is moisture and vapor proof. Seal the wrapping with freezer tape and label and date each sandwich. Avoid using tin foil, for it can easily tear, exposing the sandwich to the possibility of "freezer burn."

■ Do freeze sliced meat, chicken, fish, nut butters, and cooked bean spreads.

■ Bind frozen sandwich spreads with fruit juice, applesauce, non-fat yogurt, catsup, or mustard. They freeze well, and allow you to avoid the fat in mayonnaise.

■ Don't freeze watery raw vegetables such as lettuce, tomatoes, celery, or cucumbers. Avoid freezing hard-cooked egg white, for when it thaws it turns to "sog."

Sandwich and Sandwich Spread Recipes

THE PEANUT BUTTER PRESCRIPTION

Peanut butter, that grand old classic, was invented by a nutrition-conscious physician as a high-protein prescription for his patients. It has become a staple in most households with children. While nuts contain no cholesterol, they are generally high in fats. They should be considered a main dish and eaten sparingly, not as a casual snack food.

When using the peanut butter "remedy," be sure to check the label of the brand you buy. Some peanut butter on supermarket shelves is loaded with sugar and salt. If you discover that the peanut oil has risen to the top of the jar, simply pour it out, and avoid eating the extra fat.

Store peanut butter in the refrigerator to guard against its turning rancid. If you buy several jars of peanut butter at one time, keep all extras in your freezer. Be sure peanut butter is frozen in plastic containers; glass jars can become brittle and crack.

Use peanut butter straight out of the jar or make a lighter spread by combining it with non-fat yogurt or applesauce. Peanut butter can be sweetened with its standard companions, fruit preserves and honey, and also with chutney or maple syrup. The amounts can vary with your preference.

Peanut butter will happily share the stage with a variety of performers. Try the following combinations and invent some of your own.

- Add a layer of thinly sliced apples or oranges and top with a crisp lettuce leaf.

- Sprinkle the sandwich with chopped pitted prunes or dates.

- Dot with raisins and chopped celery.

- Layer with red bell pepper and thinly sliced cucumbers.

- Sprinkle with grated carrots and alfalfa sprouts.

- Dot with thinly sliced radishes.

- Layer with sliced bananas and sliced seedless grapes.

- Add thinly sliced red onion and tomato along with a handful of alfalfa sprouts.

- Layer with crushed, drained pineapple.

- Add a layer of fresh or frozen blueberries or raspberries.

ORANGE PEANUT BUTTER SANDWICH

Mix 2 Tb. peanut butter with 2 Tb. orange juice concentrate. Spread onto a slice of bread. Dot with sliced bananas and top with second slice of bread.

GARBANZO LEMON SPREAD

1 can garbanzo beans (15-1/2 oz.), drained; reserve liquid

Juice from half a lemon

1 green onion, chopped

2 Tb. parsley, chopped

1 to 2 cloves garlic, chopped

Combine drained garbanzo beans, lemon juice, green onion, parsley, and garlic in food processor. If mixture is too thick, thin with 1-2 Tb. liquid reserved from garbanzo beans. Process until smooth. This spread also makes a good vegetable dip. Yields about 1-1/2 cups spread.

LENTIL-LIME SPREAD

1/2 cup lentils

1 small carrot, grated

2 tsp. peeled, minced ginger

2 cups water

4 Tb. frozen apple juice concentrate, thawed

1/2 cup raisins

1 tsp. cinnamon

Juice of 1/2 lime

1/3 cup apple juice

Toasted bread

Honey (optional)

Cook lentils, carrot, and ginger in water and apple juice concentrate for 30 minutes at medium-low heat. Add raisins and cinnamon. Continue cooking until lentils are tender and raisins are plump—about 5 minutes. Mix lentil mixture, lime juice, and apple juice in a food processor or blender until coarsely blended. Spread toast with honey and add lentil-lime spread. Yields about 1-1/2 cups spread.

BUTTERNUT SQUASH PANCAKE SANDWICH

Here is a special pancake recipe for a weekend breakfast; the extras can be used for weekday lunches. Cowboys in the Wild West took leftover flapjacks and stuffed them into their pockets for eating out on the range. Your child can also enjoy this hearty meal.

1 small butternut squash

2 egg whites

1/2 cup non-fat milk or water

1 cup whole-wheat pastry flour

1 cup unbleached white flour

2 tsp. baking powder

1/2 tsp. salt

1/2 tsp. ground cinnamon

1/4 tsp. ground nutmeg

Preheat oven to 350 degrees. Bake squash for 40 minutes, or until tender when pierced with a fork. Peel, seed, mash, and let cool. Add egg whites and milk or water to squash and mix well. In a separate bowl stir together flours, baking powder, salt, cinnamon, and nutmeg. Add dry mixture to squash. Lightly spray a non-stick skillet with vegetable oil. Pour in 1/4 cup squash mixture per pancake and cook over medium heat about 3-4 minutes. Flip pancakes and press down to flatten. Cook another 3-4 minutes, or until lightly browned. Repeat until all pancakes are cooked.

Wrap leftovers individually and stack them in your freezer. When you want a pancake sandwich, spread fruit preserves between two pancakes and wrap for lunch. Or simply send pancakes with a container of applesauce for lunchtime dipping. Use extra waffles to make waffle-wiches, and remember, French toast also makes interesting sandwiches. Fat-proof waffles and French toast by using egg whites and non-fat milk in your recipes. Makes 13 pancakes.

GARDEN SANDWICH

This sandwich is a favorite at our house. Spread whole-grain bread with mustard. Layer with the following:

> Cucumbers, peeled and thinly sliced
>
> Red bell peppers, sliced
>
> Tomato, sliced
>
> Shredded carrot (optional)
>
> Lettuce leaf

Top with second slice of bread.

CONFETTI EGG-WHITE SANDWICH

Each morning Josh took two fresh eggs from the family chicken coop. They were carefully carried to school and presented to the cafeteria cook who enjoyed them for breakfast. Josh was rewarded with a free lunch. Present-day food research suggests that egg yolk is no joke, containing 260 milligrams of cholesterol.

> 2 hard-cooked egg whites; discard the yolks
>
> 2 Tb. finely chopped red pepper
>
> 1 Tb. chopped green onion
>
> 1 Tb. sweet pickle relish

1 tsp. Dijon mustard

Dash of turmeric

Mash egg white with a fork. Mix in remaining ingredients. This is a good filling for pocket bread. Garnish with lettuce and thinly sliced tomato. Yields 1-2 servings.

SCRAMBLED TOFU SANDWICH

At first glance, tofu doesn't turn heads. A tofu square looks like a cake of soap and has the flavor of chalky milk. Unadorned, it is like pizza without topping. But dress tofu up, and you can make it a top attraction in the lunch box.

1/2 green pepper, chopped

1 green onion, chopped

1 tsp. soy sauce

8 oz. tofu

Turmeric (enough to turn tofu a light golden color)

Garlic powder

Cut tofu into slices; pat dry. Mash with fork. Saute green pepper and onion in soy sauce until they begin to soften. Add tofu to skillet and season with a sprinkle of turmeric and garlic powder. Turmeric will turn tofu yellow, giving the appearance of scrambled eggs. Spread bread with mustard and garnish with lettuce and thin slices of tomato. Yields 2-3 servings.

CHICKEN APPLE SPREAD

1 cup chopped cooked seasoned chicken (or half a medium-sized chicken breast)

2 Tb. plain non-fat yogurt

1 tsp. minced parsley or basil

2 to 4 Tb. apple juice

Mix ingredients in food processor. Spread on whole-grain bread. Yields about 3-4 servings.

TURKEY AND CRANBERRIES

Place thinly sliced turkey on bread. Spread cranberry sauce over the turkey and top with a crisp lettuce leaf and second slice of bread.

SARDINE LEMON SPREAD

Mary was the new student in school, and her mother packed Mary's favorite sandwich for her first day in class. At lunchtime she unwrapped this special treat; the strong aroma of sardines spread through the room. The shout "Who brought fish?" roared through the air. Mary rushed to the garbage can to dispose of the smelly evidence. Make sure your child has a few lunchtime friends before packing sardines.

 1 can sardines (3-3/4 oz.), water packed, drained

 1 Tb. chopped onion

 1/2 tsp. Dijon mustard

 1 tsp. grated lemon rind

 1 Tb. lemon juice

 1 Tb. parsley

Mash sardines and mix together with remaining ingredients. Spread onto bread, and if you feel daring, garnish with thin apple slices.

FISH SPREAD

This is a good way to use that extra piece of fish that always seems to be left over from dinner.

 1 cup seasoned boneless, cooked fish fillet

 1/2 small onion, finely chopped

 1/2 tsp. nutmeg

 1/2 celery stalk, chopped

 2 Tb. parsley, minced

1/4 cup lemon juice

1 to 3 Tb. non-fat yogurt or catsup. (enough to moisten mixture; amounts can vary)

1/4 Tb. dill

Blend ingredients together, spread on bread, and garnish with your favorite veggies.

TUNA PINEAPPLE SPREAD

Tuna spreads are simple to prepare.

1 can tuna (6-1/2 oz.), packed in water, drained

2 Tb. orange juice

2 Tb. unsweetened applesauce

1/2 tsp. prepared mustard

2 Tb. non-fat yogurt

1/4 cup crushed pineapple, drained

Combine ingredients in a medium bowl. Yields about 1-1/2 cups.

BREAD STUFFER

For your teenager, this sandwich works best with crusty dark or French bread rolls. Slice off the end of the bread roll and pull out the soft interior, which you can save for bread crumbs. Fill the interior with marinated bean salad, or marinated cooked vegetables. (see low-fat recipes in Chapter 6). Replace the cut end and wrap the loaf in plastic wrap. By lunchtime, the flavors from the filling will have deliciously saturated the bread. Eat the salad with a fork and then enjoy the edible container.

FALAFEL BURGERS WITH DRESSING

Falafel is a spicy garbanzo-bean powder that you can buy in most supermarkets and natural-foods stores.

Mix 1 cup of falafel with 3/4 cup water. Let stand 10 minutes. When ready to use mixture, it should be about the consistency of cookie dough. If it is too thick, simply add more water.

Form "dough" into 3-inch patties and cook until golden brown in a non-stick skillet for about 3 minutes on each side. Chill and stuff burger into pocket bread with lettuce, tomato, and a thin slice of red onion. Yields 5-6 burgers. Send a small container of dressing (recipe below).

FALAFEL DRESSING

1 cup non-fat plain yogurt

1 clove garlic, minced

1 tsp. soy sauce

1 Tb. parsley, minced

Combine ingredients in a bowl. Pack dressing in a small container to add to the pocket sandwich at lunchtime.

WHITE BEAN AND HERB SPREAD

Rose's school was near the ocean, and the playground was often full of uninvited guests. Enormous sea gulls arrived from the beach for lunch. Rose's mother never knew how often the lunch she packed was fed to the visitors. Don't pack a lunch for the birds. Win your child's approval with the creaminess of beans in this spread topped with the crunchy texture of cucumber.

1 cup canned and drained white beans

2 Tb. chopped parsley

1 tsp. dried dill

1 clove garlic, chopped

1/8 tsp. pepper

1 Tb. fresh lemon juice

Sliced cucumber

Combine beans, parsley, dill, garlic, pepper, and lemon juice in a food processor until smooth. Taste for seasoning. Spread mixture on toasted bread. Layer with cucumber and top with another slice of bread. Makes enough for 3-4 sandwiches.

APPLE AND SWEET POTATO SANDWICH SPREAD

1 cup baked, peeled, and mashed sweet potato

1 medium-sized apple, peeled and diced

Pinch of ground allspice

1/2 tsp. cinnamon

1 tsp. lemon juice

1/4 cup minced onion

1/4 cup apple juice

Mix together sweet potato, apple, allspice, cinnamon, and lemon juice. Saute onion in apple juice until soft. Mix together. Spread on toasted bread or rice cakes. Makes enough for 3-4 sandwiches.

Natural Nibbles

CHAPTER 6

Children's tastes are heavily influenced by television advertising. Mostly, it is high-fat and sugary snacks that children see. The command "Eat your vegetables!" is as frightening as the monster from Saturday-morning cartoons.

If the only vegetables your children have ever seen are limp zucchini and murky-looking spinach, it's no wonder they think "green things" are yucky. Soft, mealy apples are not on any kid's favorite-foods list either. The fear of strangeness in food is practically universal among children, and many researchers believe it has a built-in genetic basis.

Whether you pick your fruits and vegetables from the supermarket or right out of the garden, choose produce that is fresh.

Use the Following Tips to Help Get a "Yes" Vote in Your Fruit and Vegetable Campaign

■ Children usually prefer vegetables that are slightly undercooked, crunchy, and bright in color.

■ Raw vegetables are often more popular with kids than when cooked, and they require almost zero preparation time.

■ Take time to cut veggies carefully. The more eye-appealing you make them, the more tempting they become.

■ Peeling vegetables is a waste of time and nutrients. When you're in a hurry, rely on "ready-cut" vegetables found in the produce section and frozen-food department of your supermarket. If frozen, let them thaw in the lunch box.

■ Expand youngsters' horizons beyond carrot sticks with a changing array of choices. A few cherry tomatoes, green pea pods, and radish roses might disappear more quickly than a baggie filled with pale celery.

■ Rub corn with lemon juice and sprinkle lightly with salt. Children love corn on the cob, but fresh corn is only available in the summer. During the school year, pack cooked fresh-frozen corn on the cob.

■ Pack chunks of fruit on toothpicks for dipping in sweetened non-fat yogurt, or applesauce flavored with cinnamon. Sprinkle cut fruit with lemon juice to avoid discoloration.

- Do something daring like packing slices of kiwi, mango, pomegranate, papaya, or star fruit.

- Make fruit "truffles." Stuff pitted prunes, dates, or dried apricot halves with chutney.

Dips

Who says dips are just for chips, and only for snacks? Fruits and vegetables are hard to pass up when they are accompanied by a container of dip.

BEAN DIP

Served with crusty whole-wheat bread or pieces of pocket bread, celery sticks, and broccoli and cauliflower florets, you have just about a complete meal.

   1 cup canned non-fat vegetarian refried beans

   2 Tb. mild salsa

   1 tsp. chili powder or a splash of tabasco sauce

   1/2 tsp. cumin powder

Blend ingredients in a small bowl. If mixture is too thick for easy dipping, add more mild salsa to thin. Yields 2 cups.

SWEET PEA DIP

Send with baked tortilla chips and crunchy carrot sticks.

   2-1/2 cups frozen green peas, thawed

   2 Tb. lemon juice

   1/2 cup red onion

   1-1/2 tsp. minced garlic

1 tsp. ground cumin

2 Tb. mild salsa or 1 tsp. Tabasco sauce

Puree all ingredients in blender until smooth. Yields 2-1/2 cups.

HONEY YOGURT DIP

Apple chunks, orange slices, kiwi rounds, and bananas are great dipped in this sweet and simple sauce.

1 cup non-fat yogurt

2 Tb. honey

1 tsp. vanilla

1/2 tsp. grated nutmeg

Combine ingredients. Chill and pack.

The Salad Bar

School cafeterias find lunchtime salad bars are popular with kids. Packing salads at home for lunch boxes can be a way to combine fruits and vegetables with bits and pieces of leftovers to make hearty main dishes. Last night's steamed potatoes can become the base for a lunch-box potato salad.

Children like to see what they're eating, so avoid "glopping" up their salads with gobs of dressing. The key to tempting lettuce salads is crispness. So send the dressing in a separate container for lunchtime mixing.

The word "sundae" can mean more than ice cream covered with chocolate sauce. Create salad sundaes by packing tempting toppings that can be sprinkled on at lunchtime: baked whole-wheat croutons, baked tortilla chips, raisins, chopped fruit, and popcorn. (Make homemade tortilla chips by cutting soft corn tortillas into pieces and baking them on a baking sheet in single layers at 275 degrees for 10-15 minutes until crisp.) Homemade baked chips are a fraction of the cost of store-bought chips. If you're lucky enough to find freshly made tortillas in your grocery, you'll have an especially delicious treat.

Keep your eyes open for international salad combinations from restaurant menus and in the aisles of your favorite ethnic grocery or gourmet deli. Substitute non-fat yogurt or non-fat salad dressing in salads that you find dripping with mayonnaise or oil.

THE INTERNATIONAL SALAD BAR

■ Mexican Corn Salad: 2 cups fresh-frozen corn kernels, thawed; 1/2 cup tomato, chopped; 2 cloves garlic, minced; 1/2 cucumber, peeled and chopped; 2 Tb. parsley, chopped; 2 Tb. cilantro, chopped; 1/2 green pepper, chopped; 1/4 tsp. oregano; and a splash of oil-free dressing. You'll find many new oil-free dressings in your supermarket. This salad takes five minutes to prepare.

■ Middle Eastern Tabouli is a lunch-box salad to start the night before. Put one-half cup bulgur wheat in a bowl, and pour 1 cup boiling water over it. Let it stand for about an hour. Drain any remaining water. Refrigerate overnight. In the morning add tomato chunks, 1/2 cup chopped parsley, a pinch of dried mint, 2 Tb. lemon juice, 1/4 cup chopped green onions, and 1/2 cup cooked garbanzo beans.

■ Sweet East Indian Curry: 1-1/2 cups cooked brown rice, 2 sliced pitted prunes, 1/4 cup raisins, 1/4 cup unsweetened crushed pineapple, 1/2 cup applesauce, 1/4 tsp. cinnamon, 1/2 tsp. curry, 1 Tb. chutney (optional). Combine ingredients and chill before packing.

■ Hawaiian Fruit Salad is always a winner. In fall and winter, toss together green and red apple chunks, unpeeled for color, orange and pineapple pieces, and raisins. Dress with a squeeze of lemon juice to keep fruit from discoloring.

■ Try Brazilian Banana Salad made with sliced bananas, seedless grapes, and chopped dates, dressed with non-fat raspberry or peach yogurt.

■ For a Japanese Rice Salad, use 1-1/2 cups brown rice as the background for this jewel-encrusted combination. Mix rice with a cup of fresh or frozen blanched vegetables. Use carrots, peas, broccoli, corn, or your child's favorites. Add halved cherry tomatoes and sliced water chestnuts. Dress with a mixture of 1 Tb. lemon juice, 1 Tb. apple cider vinegar, 1 tsp. soy sauce, and 2 tsp. honey. Top with a sprinkling of chopped red sweet peppers. (Cooked rice keeps well in the refrigerator for as long as two weeks. It's great to have on hand for a quick meal.)

■ Create an African Salad with cold seasoned chicken, kidney beans, tomato chunks, red pepper slivers, and a squeeze of lemon juice. Season with a pinch of cumin and mint.

OODLES OF NOODLES

Noodles come in a merry-go-round of unusual shapes and make a great platform for creating delicious salads. Italian pasta salads are fun to make with shells, bows, twists, tubes, and wheels. Try using Japanese soba noodles. Add colored noodles made partly from powdered vegetables. Combine cooked noodles with a handful of frozen stir-fry vegetables that have been blanched in boiling water for two minutes and cooled under cold running water. This cooking method keeps vegetables crisp and the colors bright. Dress your noodle creations with oil-free Italian dressing.

TUNA PASTA SALAD

1-1/2 cups cooked noodle shells or spirals

1/2 cup plain non-fat yogurt

1-1/2 tsp. honey

1 Tb. lemon juice

1/2 tsp. Balsamic vinegar

1/2 tsp. dill

1/4 tsp. paprika

6 oz. can tuna, packed in water

1/3 cup frozen peas

1/4 chopped red pepper

2 Tb. green onion, chopped

Mix ingredients together in a large bowl. Chill before packing. Yields 4 servings.

ALL-AMERICAN THREE-BEAN SALAD

This salad takes about as much effort as opening three cans. You can make this for lunch, and there's plenty left over to get a head start on dinner.

8 oz. can lima beans

8 oz. can kidney beans

8 oz. can green beans

1/4 cup apple cider vinegar

2 Tb. honey

1/4 cup water

2 Tb. frozen apple juice concentrate

3 Tb. minced onion

3 Tb. minced parsley

1 tomato, diced

Open the cans and drain the beans. Combine beans in a large bowl. Stir vinegar, honey, water, and apple juice concentrate together in a small bowl. Pour vinegar mixture over beans and mix well. Add onion, parsley, and tomato. Chill before packing. Three-Bean Salad tastes best if you refrigerate it overnight. Store the unopened cans in the refrigerator so the salad will be cold when you make it. Yields about four 1-cup servings.

JICAMA-ORANGE-MINT-SALAD

Jicama is a crunchy root vegetable popular in South America. If your family likes water chestnuts, they'll love jicama.

2 to 3 cups jicama, peeled and sliced into bite-sized pieces

1 tsp. dried mint

1/3 cup orange juice

1 navel orange, peeled and diced

Pinch of salt

Combine ingredients in a medium bowl. Chill and pack for a refreshing lunchtime salad. Yields 3-4 servings.

MARINATED VEGGIES

Marinated vegetables are a tasty variation. Loosely pack steamed vegetables into a glass container. Add a marinade. Screw the lid on tightly, and tilt jar around until veggies are well coated. Let them marinate overnight. Remove from marinade before packing. They're great for lunchtime finger food.

MARINADE

Here is an easy recipe for a sweet-and-sour marinade. It can also be used as a salad dressing.

1/2 cup balsamic vinegar

Juice of one lemon

1/4 to 1/2 tsp. prepared mustard

1 garlic clove, mashed

1 to 2 tsp. minced fresh ginger

Honey, to taste

Whirl ingredients in a blender. Taste for sweetness. If necessary, add more honey.

NEW POTATO SALAD

The secret to this tasty salad is adding the dressing while the potatoes are still warm. You can eat this salad for breakfast, lunch, or dinner.

10 small new red potatoes, unpeeled

Water for boiling

4 Tb. balsamic vinegar

1/2 tsp. prepared mustard

1 small red or green pepper, diced

1 tsp. dried dill

1/2 tsp. dried rosemary

2 green onions, chopped

Salt

Pepper

In a medium saucepan, cook potatoes in water until tender and drain. In a small bowl, combine vinegar and mustard. Add red or green pepper, dill, rosemary, and green onions. Pour vinegar mixture over warm potatoes. Add salt and pepper to taste. Chill and pack for lunchtime eating.

Meals on the Go

A friend once remarked happily that she loves preparing meals from leftovers. Because there is so little work involved, she feels like a guest at her own table. Cooking enough food for dinner to provide leftovers for tomorrow's lunch box is another way to make yourself feel as though you have help in the kitchen.

You'll find recipes in this chapter that are easy to assemble on the spot as well as recipes that must be prepared ahead. Make them for side dishes with dinner, and use the extras in the lunch box.

EARLY BIRD MILLET MEDLEY

Millet is a small, round, golden grain. Many people think of it only as bird seed. It's for birds and people too. This medley will make everyone sing.

> 1 cup millet
>
> 4 cups water
>
> 1/4 cup soy sauce
>
> 1 onion, chopped
>
> 1 large garlic clove, minced
>
> 1-1/2 carrots, chopped
>
> 1/2 red pepper, chopped (optional)
>
> 2 celery stalks, chopped
>
> 1 medium potato, peeled and cut into bite-sized chunks
>
> 1 tsp. rosemary
>
> 1/4 tsp. cayenne pepper
>
> 1 cup frozen peas

Boil 4 cups water and add millet, soy sauce, onion, garlic, carrots, celery, red pepper, potato, rosemary, and cayenne pepper. Reduce heat and simmer, covered, for 30-35 minutes. Remove from heat and stir in the peas. Chill before packing. Yields 7 cups.

OVEN-BAKED DRUMSTICKS

Chicken drumsticks are easy to make and easy to eat. Make a batch the night before for fast lunch packing in the morning. They're great for after-school snacks too.

1/2 cup whole-wheat flour

1/4 tsp. paprika

1/4 tsp. salt

1/4 tsp. pepper

1/4 tsp. garlic powder (optional)

8 chicken legs, with skin removed

1/2 cup non-fat milk

1 egg white, beaten

1/2 to 1 cup Grapenuts, cornmeal, or polenta

Preheat oven to 375 degrees. Put flour, paprika, salt, pepper, and garlic powder into sturdy, clean paper bag and shake it to mix ingredients. Wash and dry the chicken legs and shake them in the flour mixture. Beat milk and egg white together. Dip chicken in milk mixture, then roll the chicken in Grapenuts, corn meal, or polenta. Bake for 45-55 minutes, or until done. Cool, wrap individually, and freeze. When added to the lunch box, they will thaw by noon.

BLACK BEAN CHILI

1/4 cup diced onion

1 clove garlic

1/2 tsp. oil

1 tsp. cumin

1 tsp. chili powder

1 cup canned stewed tomatoes

1 16-oz. can black beans

1/4 cup frozen corn

1/2 tsp. oregano

1/4 cup mild salsa

1 tsp. cilantro

1 Tb. cornmeal

Saute onion and garlic in oil for 3 minutes. Add cumin and chili powder. Continue cooking until onion is transparent. Add tomatoes, black beans, corn, oregano, salsa, and cilantro. Cook on medium heat for 15 minutes. Add cornmeal. Reduce heat and simmer for 10 minutes. Add salt to taste.

THE FLOPPY DISK

Served hot or cold, pizza is at the top of nearly every kid's favorite-foods list. Pizza can be a great way to add vegetables to your child's meals. Load it with mushrooms, red bell peppers, rings of onions, shredded zucchini, and tomatoes. Commercially prepared pizza is usually overflowing with rivers of cheese, which is high in fat. Here is a way to make your own pizza with part-skim mozzarella cheese used as a condiment. Pizza without cheese is also delicious. Use whole-grain English muffins, a circle of pocket bread, or a slice of bread trimmed into a circle for the pizza base.

Spread a pizza base with pizza sauce or prepared spaghetti sauce, and top with a combination of veggies. Check your refrigerator for leftover cooked vegetables that would make tasty toppings. Sprinkle your creation with dried basil, oregano, and chopped parsley. Top with a light toss of part-skim mozzarella cheese. Broil until cheese melts. Chill and wrap.

ROSY RICE

Kids are notorious for eating cold leftover pizza and spaghetti straight out of the refrigerator. Here is another hot dish that is delicious eaten chilled.

1 onion, chopped

1 red or green pepper, diced

2 cloves garlic, minced

4 cups vegetable broth

28-oz. can stewed tomatoes

2 cups brown rice

1/4 cup chopped parsley

1 cup frozen corn

Saute onion, red or green pepper, and garlic in 1/4 cup vegetable broth until soft. Add remaining vegetable broth and stewed tomatoes. Bring liquid to a boil, add rice, and reduce heat to simmer for 45 minutes. Remove from heat, add parsley and frozen corn. Chill before packing. For an extra treat, scoop rice into a green pepper that has been cut in half. Wrap and send. Yields about six servings.

ANYTIME CEREAL

For the child who loves cereal, you can make a quick easy-to-prepare lunch by packing a favorite whole-grain cereal in an unbreakable container. Send it to school with a chilled thermos of low-fat milk or apple juice to add at lunchtime. Or pack a cereal sundae topped with non-fat yogurt and slices of fresh or dried fruit.

Bravo Burrito

Kids love eating with their hands, and tortillas make it socially acceptable. Use thin, soft, pliable, eight-inch flour tortillas. Read labels when buying tortillas, for the fat content varies among brands. Look for tortillas with less than two grams of fat per serving. Tortillas are great for filling with all kinds of burrito variations. Burrito packages don't always have to mean beans.

SWEET AND SPICY BEAN BURRITO

1/4 cup non-fat vegetarian refried beans

1/4 cup mashed cooked sweet potato or baked butternut squash

Dash of cumin

Salsa

Lettuce (optional)

Tomato (optional)

Soft 8-inch flour tortilla

Combine beans, sweet potato, and spices. Spread mixture down the middle of a tortilla and top with salsa, lettuce, and tomato. Fold over the opposing edges of the circle. Next, fold over the remaining two edges to complete the envelope. Wrap immediately. Yields 2 servings.

TEXAS BAR-B-QUE BURRITO

Soft 8-inch flour tortilla

Lettuce

1/4 cup canned vegetarian baked beans

1 tsp. catsup

1/2 tsp. mustard

Thinly sliced tomato

Place lettuce in center of tortilla. Spoon on beans. Add catsup, mustard, and tomato. Fold over opposing edges of the circle. Next, fold over the remaining two edges to complete the envelope. Wrap immediately.

Rainbow Drinks

CHAPTER 8

Children need liquid to replace the normal water lost during a busy, active day. The long-handled dipper and the old oaken bucket that sat in the corner of the one-room schoolhouse to quench thirst has been replaced by rainbow-colored thermos bottles and drinks to match.

Let's begin with nature's most natural drink... water.

Just like a growing plant, your child needs water to survive. The body itself is made up of fifty to seventy-five percent water. Water contains no additives, preservatives, or empty calories. In fact, it's calorie free. It is inexpensive, contains trace minerals, and satisfies the body's need for liquid. The life-sustaining properties of water are second only to air in importance to the body. Although water doesn't have the sizzle of soda pop, when your child is thirsty, there's nothing like it.

Finding a refreshing drink of water at school is not always simple. Classroom fountains are busy places, usually combined with a sink that is often filled with paintbrushes that need cleaning or gooey half-used cups of wheat paste, and holidays find sink and fountain drains closed with glitter and glue. A vacuum bottle of iced water with a twist of lemon can be a welcome surprise in your child's lunch box.

HERB TEAS

Peter Rabbit was served tea by his mother when he returned from Mr. McGregor's garden. You too can send selected caffeine-free herb teas for a lunchtime treat. Try cinnamon rose, peppermint, or sweet orange spice. Send it either hot or chilled in a vacuum jar.

JUICE MENU—RIPE FOR BLENDING

Apple	Grapefruit	Pear	Carrot	Banana
Pineapple	Apricot	Tomato	Cranberry	Strawberry
Mango	Prune	Grape	Orange	Cherry

If your children clamor for artificially flavored canned drinks, blend two or three natural juices together for more exotic flavors. Apple juice is a friendly mixer and combines well with many flavors. You can add extra zing with a squeeze of lemon or lime, a shake of cinnamon, or a drop of vanilla or mint extract. Fresh or frozen fruit can be added to drinks for additional taste and thickness. Mix 1 cup of fruit with 1 cup of juice in your blender. Create your own "house-specialty," like Patty's Punch, or Strawberry Dynamite.

Mix It Up! Blended Juice Drinks

CRANBERRY SUNRISE

1/4 cup cranberry juice

1 cup orange juice

1/2 cup pineapple juice

Combine all ingredients and stir until blended.

CARROT COOLER

1 cup carrot juice

1/2 cup tomato juice

Squeeze of lemon

Combine ingredients and stir until blended.

APRICOT EXPRESS

1/2 cup apricot nectar

1/3 cup apple juice

Combine ingredients and stir until blended.

(The following recipes require a blender.)

HAWAIIAN HOLIDAY

1 cup pineapple juice

1 ripe banana

1 cup fresh or frozen strawberries

Combine ingredients and blend until smooth.

ORANGE SMOOTHIE

1 cup orange juice

1 cup papaya or fresh or frozen raspberries

1/3 cup non-fat powdered dry milk

Combine ingredients, blend until smooth.

PEAR PUNCH

1 cup apple juice

1 peeled, sliced pear

Shake of cinnamon

Combine ingredients, blend until smooth.

SALAD SHAKE

1 cup low-salt tomato juice

1 carrot, sliced

1/2 green pepper

1 Tb. chopped parsley

Squeeze of lemon

Combine ingredients, blend until smooth.

BANANA SHAKE

1 banana

1 cup orange juice

1/2 tsp. vanilla

1 Tb. honey

Combine ingredients, blend until smooth.

Yummy Yogurt Drinks

Non-fat yogurt shakes can be meals in themselves. They can be made thick enough to eat with a spoon, or thin enough to drink. Yogurt originated as a way to preserve milk, and it keeps well in the lunch box. To thicken yogurt drinks, add fresh or frozen fruit; to thin, add fruit juice. Combine all ingredients, blend until smooth.

SAUCY APPLE

1/2 cup non-fat, plain yogurt

1/2 cup apple juice

1/2 cup applesauce

1/8 tsp. cinnamon

TROPICAL ISLAND

1/2 cup plain non-fat yogurt

1 cup unsweetened pineapple juice

1 cup strawberries, fresh or frozen

1/8 tsp. vanilla

Flavored Milk

(For each of the following recipes, combine ingredients in a blender and blend until smooth.)

STRAWBERRY SHAKE

1 cup non-fat milk

1 cup fresh or frozen berries

1/4 tsp. vanilla

ORANGE COOLER

1 cup non-fat milk

1 to 3 Tb. orange juice concentrate

1/4 tsp. vanilla

PURPLE COW

1 cup non-fat milk

1 to 3 Tb. frozen grape juice concentrate

Desserts

CHAPTER 9

Children expect dessert with lunch. Keep your brown-baggers happy by including dessert made with well-chosen ingredients that add to nutritional needs and avoid the problem of empty calories and excessive fat.

Remember that not all desserts need to be complicated; muffins and quick breads are good lunch-box treats. You'll find many of the recipes in this chapter good enough to eat anywhere along the lunch line-up, before the main course as well as after it.

More than 4,000 years ago Egyptian mothers used whole-grain flours, seeds, and dried fruits when making desserts. You too can make similar nutritious sweet-treats by adding dried apricots, figs, snipped dates, pitted prunes, or raisins to your cake and cookie batters.

You can add exotic flavors to your baking year-round with fresh, frozen, or canned fruits. Try adding frozen blueberries, canned unsweetened pineapple, or chopped fresh apples. The addition of fresh grated zucchini or carrots is a way to dress up vegetables in party clothes, and make them acceptable for some children. Try substituting applesauce for some of the fat called for in your favorite cake and cookie recipes. Many prepackaged cake mixes will accept applesauce in place of oil. Most fruit and vegetable cakes and cookies freeze well, and many basic recipes will gladly welcome your naturally sweet additions.

If your family is accustomed to sweet foods, and you'd like to cut back on sugar, begin slowly by decreasing the sugar each time you make a recipe. Many recipes can easily stand having the sugar cut in half and still taste sweet. Apple juice concentrate is a potent sweetener and can be used to replace sugar in some recipes. When using fruit juices in baking, add 1/4 to 1/2 tsp. baking soda per cup of juice to avoid an acid taste in what you make. Most children prefer two helpings of dessert. Make your servings small so that it's easy to say yes to seconds.

You may find it surprising that many brands of baking powder contain aluminum. Researchers are finding excessive aluminum may be harmful to the brain. Look for aluminum-free baking powder.

With the call "Batter up," parents and children can easily use team-effort baking ideas to fill the home plate for next day's lunch box. Use your favorite recipes and package your own dry cake and cookie mixes. Store them in separate plastic bags in your freezer. Include directions for completing the recipe, and if your children are old enough, add them to your baking team. All your child needs to do is add a few liquid ingredients and bake.

"Out of sight, out of mind" is a ploy that helps packed treats last longer. I know one energetic mother who hides cookies in the backyard barbecue, while another friend, and mother of four teenage boys, hides lunch-box treats under her bed. Try wrapping your desserts individually and stashing them in your freezer.

Keep some nutritious desserts handy for mornings when your family is running late, and let everyone grab a handful on the way out the door for a nutritious breakfast on the run.

GORILLA GRAHAMS

Here is a quick-fix dessert when the cookie jar is empty and time is short. The crisp cracker and creamy filling make great partners. This is a sizeable, satisfying, low-fat treat.

> 1 ripe banana, mashed
>
> 1 tsp. fresh lemon juice
>
> 2 tsp. applesauce
>
> 6 graham crackers

In a medium bowl, mash banana with a fork. Add lemon juice and applesauce. Break graham crackers in half. Frost half of the square with the banana mixture and place the other half cracker on top. Wrap individually and freeze. Send them to school frozen. Yields 6 servings.

BLUEBERRY ORANGE MUFFINS

1 cup whole-wheat flour

3/4 cup unbleached white flour

1-1/2 tsp. baking powder

1/2 tsp. cinnamon

1 Tb. orange rind, chopped

2 egg whites

1/4 cup vegetable oil

1/2 tsp. baking soda

1 cup orange juice

1/4 cup brown sugar

1-1/2 cups blueberries, fresh or fresh frozen

Preheat oven to 375 degrees. In a large bowl, mix together flours, baking powder, cinnamon, and orange rind. In a smaller bowl, beat together egg whites, oil, baking soda, orange juice, and brown sugar. Add blueberries. Stirring gently, combine liquid ingredients with the flour mixture. Fill 12 cupcake or muffin tins, lightly sprayed with vegetable oil, about two-thirds full with batter. Bake 20-30 minutes.

POPPYSEED CORN CAKE

1 cup corn meal

1 cup whole-wheat flour

2 Tb. poppy seeds

1 tsp. baking powder

1 cup carrots, shredded

1/4 cup honey

1 cup non-fat milk

2 egg whites

2 Tb. vegetable oil

Preheat oven to 400 degrees. Mix together dry ingredients. Add remaining ingredients. Pour into a 9" x 5" loaf pan that has been lightly sprayed with vegetable oil. Bake for 25-30 minutes.

APPLESAUCE SURPRISE MUFFINS

1-1/4 cups unsweetened applesauce

2 egg whites

2 Tb. vegetable oil

1/4 cup honey

1 cup whole-wheat flour

1 cup unbleached white flour

2 tsp. baking powder

3/4 tsp. baking soda

1/2 tsp. cinnamon

1/2 tsp. nutmeg

1/4 cup raisins

Strawberry jam or fruit preserves

Preheat oven to 375 degrees. In a large bowl, beat together applesauce, egg whites, oil, and honey. In a medium bowl, combine dry ingredients. Add raisins to flour mixture. Add dry ingredients to wet ingredients. Fill each section of a non-stick muffin tin half full of batter. Add 1/2 tsp. of fruit preserves to each muffin. Fill the muffin cups with the remaining batter. Bake for 20 minutes.

PUMPKIN OATMEAL COOKIES

1/3 cup brown sugar

1/3 cup honey

1/4 cup vegetable oil

2 egg whites

1 cup pumpkin puree

1 cup bleached white flour

1 cup rolled oats

1/2 tsp. baking soda

1/2 tsp. baking powder

1/2 tsp. nutmeg

1/2 tsp. cinnamon

1/2 cup raisins

Preheat oven to 400 degrees. In a large bowl, mix together brown sugar, honey, oil, egg whites, and pumpkin puree. In a medium bowl, mix together dry ingredients. Add raisins. Lightly combine wet and dry ingredients. Drop mixture by rounded teaspoonfuls about 2 inches apart onto non-stick baking sheet. Bake for about 10 minutes. Yields about 36 cookies.

BANANA-APPLE LOAF CAKE

1 cup unbleached white flour

1-1/2 cups whole-wheat flour

1 Tb. baking powder

1/4 tsp. baking soda

4 very ripe bananas, mashed

1/2 cup apple juice concentrate

2 tsp. vanilla extract

3 egg whites

2/3 cup non-fat milk

Preheat oven to 350 degrees. In a large bowl, mix together flours, baking powder, and baking soda. In a food processor, mix together bananas, apple juice, vanilla, egg whites, and non-fat milk until smooth. Pour banana mixture into flour. Do not overmix. Pour batter into 9" x 5" x 3" non-stick loaf pan that has been lightly sprayed with vegetable oil. Bake for 45 minutes. Cool and slice. Wrap slices individually and store them in your freezer. For an added attraction, cut a slice of cake into bite-sized pieces, and send a container of applesauce for dipping.

GINGERBREAD

3/4 cup dark molasses

1/4 cup honey

1/4 cup vegetable oil

1-1/4 cups orange juice

1 Tb. finely grated lemon rind

2-1/2 cups whole-wheat flour

1 tsp. baking soda

1 tsp. cinnamon

2 tsp. ground ginger

1/2 tsp. salt

1/2 cup raisins

Preheat oven to 350 degrees. In a large bowl, mix together wet ingredients. In a medium bowl, sift together dry ingredients. Add raisins. Add dry ingredients to wet ingredients. Pour into a 9" x 13" pan lightly sprayed with vegetable oil. Bake 35-40 minutes, making sure not to overbake. Gingerbread will be moist. Serves 24.

Snack
Attack

CHAPTER 10

Children usually arrive home from school with the appetites of hungry sharks. That may be the ideal time to get your child to eat raw vegetables, fresh fruit, and whole-wheat bread. Don't keep foods in the house that you don't want your children to eat. If the cookie jar is empty, your child might just turn to fruit for that after-school snack. Children will often choose nutritious food over nothing. Some researchers think children are born with an innate preference for sweets, but they will be better off not thinking every hunger pang must be fed cake.

Children are snackers with good reason. As active, growing youngsters, their caloric and nutritional needs are large in relation to body size. They have at times an adult's appetite with a child's-size stomach. Snacks are a hefty portion of a child's daily diet. More aptly, snacks might be thought of as smaller meals between larger meals. With most parents working, dinner preparation is often filled with frenzy. When mom and dad arrive home, the first question they may hear is "When's dinner?!" People are tired and tempers are short. Nutritious after-school snacks are a way to subdue hunger long enough for you to get your bearings while preparing dinner after a busy day. Children and parents have discovered that microwaves and leftovers go a long way toward answering the after-school snack question. Children quickly learn that all kinds of good things can be created for eating on the spot by simply stirring, spreading, dipping, layering, or spooning. In addition to what your child will naturally find in the refrigerator for assembling, here are some nutritious extras that you can prepare ahead as special treats for special days.

BEST BAKED APPLES

Waking up to the smell of something baking in the oven is a rare treat in today's busy work-filled world. Here is a simple recipe you can use for breakfast and chill the extras in the refrigerator for after-school snacks.

4 large green apples, cored but not peeled

1/4 cup dried figs, apricots, or pineapple, chopped (optional)

1/2 cup raisins, plumped in hot water for five minutes, then drained

1 tsp. cinnamon

1 tsp. nutmeg

1/4 cup frozen apple juice concentrate, thawed

Water

Preheat oven to 350 degrees. Place apple in a casserole dish. Combine remaining ingredients. Stuff into cavities of apples. Fill the casserole dish with water to one-fourth the height of the apples. Bake uncovered for 40 minutes, or until apples are soft and browned.

BASIC FRUIT GELATIN

It is a lovely sight to see gelatin shimmering in clear glasses on the refrigerator shelf. Using unflavored gelatin as your base, you can mix together natural combinations of flavor that will delight the whole family.

2 cups fruit juice

1 Tb. unflavored gelatin (1 Tb. gelatin will set two cups of liquid)

Mix 1/2 cup juice and 1 Tb. gelatin in medium-sized saucepan. Heat and stir until gelatin dissolves. Remove from heat. Stir in remaining juice. Pour mixture into individual serving glasses and refrigerate. For fluffy gelatin, let mixture soft-set and whirl in blender. Pour in glasses and chill.

BANANA-ORANGE GELATIN

1 Tb. unflavored gelatin

1/2 cup cold water

3 cups plain non-fat yogurt

1 large banana

1/4 cup frozen orange juice concentrate

Dissolve gelatin in 1/2 cup cold water, heating to dissolve. In blender combine yogurt, gelatin mixture, banana, and orange juice concentrate. Pour into individual glasses and refrigerate until set.

COOL SIPPING

A chilled pitcher of juice waiting on the refrigerator shelf is an invitation to drink and helps children pass up canned sodas. For small children, a small pitcher with a lid is a worthwhile investment. Children can blend their own healthful soft drinks by mixing plain mineral water or plain soda water together with juice. Carrot and celery sticks are great for stirring.

FROSTIE COOKIES

Swirl non-fat yogurt on top of a few cookies and set them in your freezer for an occasional after-school treat.

POLENTA PUDDING

Here is a delicious golden pudding made without eggs or milk. Set in clear stemmed glasses or individual dessert dishes, this sparkling treat is a nutritious after-school snack.

    1 cup frozen blueberries

    3 Tb. frozen apple juice concentrate

    2 Tb. maple syrup

    1 tsp. vanilla

    1 tsp. grated orange peel

    2-1/2 cups water

    3/4 cup polenta meal or finely ground cornmeal

In a medium bowl, combine blueberries, apple juice concentrate, maple syrup, vanilla, and orange peel. In a medium saucepan, bring water to a boil and gradually stir in polenta meal. Simmer and stir continuously for 15-20 minutes. The polenta is done when it tears away from the sides of the pot as you stir. Remove from heat and stir in blueberry mixture. Spoon into individual serving bowls and top with a drizzle of maple syrup. It's great eaten warm or chilled.

Popsicles

Homemade popsicles are a delicious freezer snack. When you make your own, the flavor combinations are almost limitless, and you don't have to settle for the dairy-rich, sugar-laden treats in the supermarket. Making your own popsicles may sound ludicrous when you barely have time to get dinner on the table until you consider they require only a few minutes of work; the freezer does the rest. Use popsicle molds if you have them, or pour the mixture into small paper cups. As a child gnaws away at the popsicle, all he or she needs to do is tear away the paper. (If you want a handle, insert a plastic spoon.) And try to avoid drinking the popsicles before they get to the freezer.

FRUIT POPS

Make fruit popsicles from any combination of your favorite juices. For variety, add fresh or stewed fruit to your juice mixture. Whirl in blender. Pour into mold and freeze.

YOGURT-ORANGE POPS

1/2 cup frozen orange juice concentrate

1 cup plain non-fat yogurt

Dash of honey, if desired

Whirl in blender. Pour into mold and freeze.

YOGURT-APPLESAUCE POPS

1 cup applesauce

1/2 cup non-fat yogurt

Honey and cinnamon to taste

Whirl in blender. Pour into mold and freeze.

STRAWBERRY-BANANA POPS

3/4 cup non-fat milk

1/4 cup instant non-fat powdered milk

1 cup strawberries

1/2 ripe banana, peeled

A few drops of vanilla

Whirl in blender. Pour into mold and freeze.

FROZEN BANANAS

These frozen delights offer cool nibbling. When frozen, they develop the taste and texture of ice cream. Select firm bananas. Cut in half crosswise so that you have two short pieces. Freeze the banana as is, or dip it into non-fat yogurt, or coat it with maple syrup and roll in Grapenuts. Insert an ice cream stick or a fat plastic straw into the sliced end. Freeze on a plate. When frozen, store in a covered container in the freezer. Grapes and canned pineapple chunks make delicious and nutritious frozen "ice cream" too.

ABOVE ALL,

ENJOY YOUR CHILDREN

FOR THESE DAYS

ONCE GONE

CAN NEVER BE

RECAPTURED.

Glossary

BROWN RICE

A grain that has been cultivated for over 4,000 years. Brown rice retains its healthful bran layer.

BULGUR

Also known as tabouli—a highly nutritious form of wheat that has been parboiled, cracked, and dried. It has a delicious nutty flavor.

CHAPATIS

A pliable flatbread made form flour, water and salt, which has excellent flavor and texture.

CHUTNEY

A condiment type relish—a combination of chopped fruits, vegetables, herbs and spices in a thick sweet-sour sauce.

CURRY POWDER

A condiment type spice from India, composed of a powder mixture of Turmeric, Coriander and other herbs and spices.

FALAFEL

Garbanzo beans or chickpeas that have been ground into a powder and mixed with herbs and spices. It is a protein rich, Middle Eastern food favorite that is gaining fast acceptance throughout the world.

GARBANZO BEANS

Also known as chickpeas, it is a bean of many uses. It can be used in salads and soups, also made into creamy sandwich spreads and dips— sometimes called hummus.

LENTIL

One of the oldest of leguminous plants. The lentil grows in pods like its botanical cousin the pea. This annual provides rich plant protein.

MILLET

Millet is probably one of our most ancient grains. It can be used as a breakfast cereal, a rice substitute, or ground coarsely and added to wheat flour for breads.

MOLASSES	The thick dark syrup that remains when sugarcane juice is boiled down and the raw sugar extracted. It is high in iron, potassium, calcium, and vitamin B.
POLENTA	Dried corn that has been ground into a meal. It is a staple in Italian kitchens.
SOBA NOODLES	A Japanese noodle made from wheat flour and buckwheat.
SOY SAUCE	An extract from fermented soybeans that is blended together with wheat or barley, salt and water to produce a spicy, slightly salty sauce.
TABOULI	(see bulgur wheat)
TOFU	A creamy, white cake made from soybean milk in a manner resembling the production of cheese. It results in an easy to digest, custard like soft cake that is high in protein and vitamin B.
WHOLE-WHEAT FLOUR	Flour made from the entire kernel of wheat.
YOGURT	A custard like food made from cultured milk, often sweetened or flavored, it has been enjoyed for thousands of years by Europeans, and now has a large following world-wide.

Bibliography

The following books helped shape my thinking for *Love in a Lunch Box*.

Bailey, C. *The Fit or Fat Target Diet*. Boston: Houghton Mifflin, 1984.

Mc Dougall, J. *The Mc Dougall Plan*. New Jersey: New Century, 1983.

Ornish, D. *Dr. Dean Ornish's Program for Reversing Heart Disease*. New York: Random House, 1990.

Pennington, J. *Food Values of Portions Commonly Used*. New York: Harper & Row, 1989.

Pritkin, N. *The Pritkin Program for Diet and Exercise*. New York: Grosset and Dunlap, 1979.

Robbins, J. *Diet for a New America*. New Hampshire: Still Point, 1987.

Index